How To Fire An Employee

The Right Way to Terminate Someone
(With Scripts, Templates, Checklists and FAQs)

KEVIN KRUSE

T.E. MILLETTE

First Edition

What is the best way to fire someone?

How can you do a hard thing, the right way?

You will learn:

- The 6 *legal* reasons to terminate someone
- A step-by-step plan for terminating an employee (telling them is Step 3)
- What to actually say (i.e., the script) when you let someone go (including the critical 12-word sentence you should *always* say first)
- What to include in a termination letter (includes sample letter you can copy)
- How to fire someone gracefully, or nicely
- The best day of the week and best time to terminate someone
- Answers to tough questions (Can you fire someone without warning? With no reason? Over the phone?)
- BONUS: Termination Checklist

FREE Management Training

At LEADx, we give busy managers FREE leadership training videos, every single day. Learn how to…

Increase Employee Engagement

Tame Your Email Inbox

Run Effective Meetings

Give Effective Feedback

More!

Get Your Free Training
www.LEADx.org

CONTENTS

How To Fire Someone The Right Way 6

The 6 Legal Reasons For Termination 8

    Reason #1 - Threats and Physical Violence 10

    Reason #2 - Theft 10

    Reason #3 - Harassment 10

    Reason #4 - Attendance 11

    Reason #5 - Insubordination 11

    Reason #6 - Incompetence 12

Step-by-Step: How To Terminate An Employee 16

    STEP ONE: Review 17

    STEP TWO: Prepare 17

    STEP THREE: Tell 18

    STEP FOUR: Escort 19

    STEP FIVE: Notify 20

What To Say When Firing Someone 22

    Step One: Tell Them 23

    Step Two: Explain Why 24

    Step Three: Explain Next Steps 24

    Step Four: Gathering Their Things 25

    Step Five: Questions 25

    Step Six: Part On Good Terms 26

    Sample Script When Firing Someone 27

How To Write A Clear Termination Letter 30

How To Fire Someone 'Nicely' 34
When Is The Best Time To Fire Someone? 37
    The Pros And Cons Of Friday 37
    The Case For Monday's 38
    What Time Of Day Should You Fire Someone? 38
    No One Right Answer 39
Can You Fire Someone Over The Phone? 41
Can You Fire Someone Without Warning? 43
    Consider Their Contract 44
    Determine If They Are "At Will" 44
    Just Because It's Legal, Doesn't Mean It's Right 44
Is It Possible To Fire Someone For No Reason? 47
Employee Termination Checklist 49
Bring the Power of LEADx Training to Your Organization 54
About the Authors 55

INTRODUCTION

How To Fire Someone The Right Way

Ask any leader and she'll agree, terminating someone's employment—having to fire someone—is the hardest thing a manager ever has to do.

When I (Kevin) was early in my career, I was absolutely horrible at it. As a small business owner, I didn't have any training on how to be a manager. I didn't have an HR department to guide me in letting someone go.

One time, I had to fire someone who wasn't performing, and because she was a friend, and I was so non-confrontational and scared, I didn't tell her that it was for poor performance. Instead, I told her it was just a layoff. It's not you, it's me... the company needs to save money.

Well that wasn't fair to them, it confused the rest of the employees—*layoffs?!*—and actually cost the company extra money as our unemployment insurance went up.

Another time I called in a sales rep to my office with the intent to fire him. He had been missing his numbers for many months and was showing no signs of improvement. What was supposed to be a termination conversation turned into an awkward back and forth debate and review of his pipeline and I agreed to give him another 60 days. Of course, it just delayed the inevitable.

This book is the guide I wish I had 25 years ago. It's never going to be easy to fire someone, and it shouldn't be. But it can be done professionally, with compassion, and in a way that actually leads to a positive relationship between both parties moving forward.

CHAPTER #1

The 6 Legal Reasons For Termination

Let's start with a warning, and I'll repeat it throughout this book.

Employment law varies greatly country to country, and state to state. You must consult with a local employment attorney. This book doesn't replace good legal counsel; consider it solid background information based on real-world experience and it will help you to explore HR issues with your lawyers more effectively.

You might be wondering if you have a good enough reason to fire someone.

- Can I fire someone if I just don't like working with them?
- How do I know if my reason is good enough that I won't get sued?
- How do I know if my reason is good enough to win in court if I *do* get sued?

When it comes to letting someone go, you should always have a specific reason. Even if your company is located in an "at will" state—where you can end employment at any time for NO reason—if you don't have a *specific* reason, you are far more likely to be accused of firing for an *illegal* reason. Illegal reasons to fire someone in the United States include letting someone go based on:

- gender
- race
- sexual orientation
- religion
- marital status
- age

Remember, the laws in your state or country may vary, and most state laws (ahem, California) are far stricter than federal laws. So we strongly recommend you talk to your HR department or to an attorney about your specific situation.

Additionally, make sure the employee in question doesn't have special protections based on a union agreement or their specific employment contract.

Having said all that, in general, there are six *legal* reasons you can fire someone.

Reason #1 - Threats and Physical Violence

If someone physically threatens or assaults a coworker, they should be fired, escorted off company grounds immediately, and the authorities should be called. In fact, you would probably be found negligent if you didn't take immediate action to protect the physical safety of your employees.

Reason #2 - Theft

Anyone who steals can be immediately terminated. This includes money (embezzlement), physical property, and also theft of intellectual property like software source code, trade secrets, or other forms of intellectual property.

Reason #3 - Harassment

Workplace harassment is considered grounds for termination. The definition of harassment? That's where it gets trickier. First of all, harassment isn't just confined to sexual harassment; it can be any kind of abusive behavior and can be between two people of the same gender. Types of harassing behavior include insults, intimidation, slurs, jokes, unwanted physical contact and even pictures.

Generally speaking, if the behavior in question is pervasive or severe enough that a reasonable person would consider it to be intimidating or abusive, it's harassment. Also, if any manager requires that someone tolerate inappropriate behavior as a condition for keeping his job, that's harassment.

Reason #4 - Attendance

From chronic lateness to not showing up at all, issues related to attendance are considered legal grounds for termination.

Like all reasons, use common sense to avoid even the appearance of a biased termination. Firing someone for being 5 minutes late one time is technically legal. But if this person files suit with a claim that the real reason is because of his age, gender or race a judge might be open to their view. If the same person was late three times, and was warned with documentation each time, you'd be on much stronger grounds.

Reason #5 - Insubordination

This can be a bit of a grey area, but in general if someone has broken company rules that they were aware of, or is willfully disobeying or disregarding legitimate instructions, it's considered insubordination and is grounds for termination.

Of course insubordination can be handled with progressive discipline, and that will be part of the context considered by a judge if you are taken to court for wrongful dismissal. Before firing someone for insubordination consider the following:

- Was the policy or instruction clearly stated?
- Did the employee understand the policy or instruction?
- Were there other workplace factors, like conflicting orders or policies, which could have confused the employee or prevented her from the proper action?
- Was any coaching or discipline attempted prior to the termination?

Reason #6 - Incompetence

Finally, the sixth legal reason to fire someone is "incompetence," which is another way of saying poor performance. This is the category that most terminations fall under. If an employee is not performing to the level you require for that role, you can fire them legally for poor performance.

Again, just because you can terminate someone for no reason, or at any time for a performance-related issue, ideally you would first take certain steps to minimize the risk of an unlawful termination lawsuit, to be fair to the employee, and to protect office morale. Ask yourself:

1) Were job expectations clearly stated?
2) Did the employee have the training and tools necessary to perform at desired level?
3) Did the employee know her performance was below required standards and that their position was at risk?
4) Did you document these performance conversations?

When it comes to documentation of your performance conversations, it doesn't have to be an official form or long report. Jotting down a note or sending an email to yourself or to your assistant is usually enough. For example, "Today (August 28, 2017) at 2:30 PM, I spoke to Jane Doe to let her know that she needs to improve her performance here as a copy editor. We need 95% of the articles she edits to contain zero typos. We discussed having her slow down while editing, or to read certain complicated articles a second time, one day later."

These notes will become helpful if you should face a wrongful termination lawsuit. It's one thing to claim "Yes, I had several performance conversations with her. No, I don't remember the dates. No I can't remember exactly what was said." Versus, "Yes, we had three conversations in three weeks. Here are the dates and times and printouts of emails that include the date stamps and notes on our conversation…"

Remember, just because you can let someone go for no reason in most states, it doesn't mean it's a good idea. Best practice is to have a specific, legal reason and documentation to back it up. When in doubt, it's best to review your decision to let someone go and the reason why with your boss or HR department.

"

Just because you can *let* someone go for no reason, doesn't mean it's a good idea.

CHAPTER #2

Step-by-Step: How To Terminate An Employee

Sure, technically you can just walk up to someone and scream, "You're fired!" But remember the big picture. Your goals should be to terminate someone and:

1) Don't disrupt normal workflow

2) Reduce risk of unnecessary legal fees and hassles from a wrongful termination lawsuit

3) Maintain a positive professional relationship with the exiting employee

While firing someone is never easy, following five basic steps will ensure that a difficult thing is being done the right way.

Remember! Employment law varies greatly country to country, and state to state. You must consult with a local employment attorney. This book doesn't replace good legal counsel; consider it solid background information

based on real-world experience and it will help you to explore HR issues with your lawyers more effectively.

STEP ONE: Review

The first step is to just pause, and to review your decision. You should never fire someone out of anger or in haste.

If you're letting someone go for performance reasons, ask yourself if they're going to be totally surprised and shocked by the news. If they are, it's a probably a sign that you could have done more to let them know they weren't meeting expectations. You should also review your decision with your boss or HR department to make sure you have proper grounds and will have their support.

STEP TWO: Prepare

The second step is to prepare for the event and the transition afterwards. Who are all the other people who will be affected by the termination?

- Do you need to coordinate with your IT or security departments?
- Who will cover this person's work in the short-term?

- Does anyone need to check for voicemail or email messages until a replacement is found?
- Will you need to quickly notify anyone outside the company, like clients or vendors they may have been interacting with?

STEP THREE: Tell

Step three is to actually tell the person they're being terminated. Do it in private, and remember to be direct and keep it short.

If they seem totally surprised and confused, you can say it's for performance reasons if it is, but you never want to use this time to rehash prior conversations, or get into a debate about their performance.

After telling them they will no longer be with the company, explain what they can expect to happen next regarding their final paycheck, benefits-related issues, and severance agreement if you're offering one.

This will be a lot for them to process in the moment. Let them know that they can ask you or the right person in HR, questions in the days and weeks ahead.

STEP FOUR: Escort

Step four is to have the person gather their personal items from their desk, turn in their keys or security badge and other company property, and to leave the building.

Standard practice is to have someone escort them at all times while they're still in the building. This is of course to protect the interests of the company; you want to prevent theft or destruction of company property (both physical property but also electronic files or emails) and minimize inappropriate behavior that would be distracting to other employees.

Some employment experts note that insisting on an escort sends the message that they can't be trusted and is not a very dignified way for someone to leave. So if the person *can* be trusted, and it's not against company policy, you could always ask them to gather their things before lunch, or before the end of the day, without the escort.

You could also suggest that they come back and meet you early the next morning or after work to gather their things. That offers them a little more privacy, and is less disruptive to the workplace.

STEP FIVE: Notify

Terminating an employee often comes as a surprise to other staff members, and can of course be quite unsettling. They'll wonder if the person quit, or was fired, or are layoffs occurring for financial reasons. So the final step in the process is to notify team members as quickly as possible.

Remember you have an obligation to protect the exiting employee's privacy, and so the less details, the better. You can just let everyone know that the terminated employee's last day was today or yesterday, that a search for a replacement has begun, and what the plans are to cover their work in the meantime.

If you are asked specific questions, you can just say something like, "For employee privacy reasons, we can't discuss the details of the situation, but feel free to reach out to me or HR privately if you need to discuss it further."

There isn't a pleasant or painless way to fire someone, but these 5 steps will minimize risk and ensure a smooth transition.

"

If someone is shocked when you fire them, you probably could have done more to let them know they weren't meeting expectations.

CHAPTER #3

What To Say When Firing Someone

Having to look someone in the eyes and tell them that they've lost their job is the hardest management thing you will ever have to do. For most people, their job is tied to their identity and, of course, is how they provide for their family. So to tell someone—someone you've worked with perhaps for a long time—they are being let go is emotionally difficult for all involved.

When I (Kevin) was younger I did it all wrong.

I'd be so scared to just come out and say it, I'd beat around the bush. I'd say, "I'm not sure this working out" or "I don't think this is the right role for you, do you?"

It was as if I thought they were going to fire themselves. Of course, they wouldn't and it would turn into a conversation about job roles and expectations and go on and on.

Other times, after blurting out that I was letting them go I'd feel compelled to make them feel better. So I'd say their work it wasn't *all* bad, and they have great potential, and we are so grateful for their service...Well that just confused them.

Another mistake I made while trying to be a "nice guy" or their friend was instead of asking them to leave the same day I'd agree to let them finish out the week. Inevitably, office productivity fell to nothing as the remaining employees heard someone was fired they'd want to talk to the person, talk with each other, gossip about what was going on, and basically it was awkward for several days. And then horrible again on the person's last day. Do you throw them a party? Take them to lunch?

Whether they are your friend, or you don't like them, whether you're firing them for poor performance or letting them go as part of a layoff, there is only one right way to give the news: **You need to do it quickly, and directly.**

Step One: Tell Them

Make sure you are having the conversation in a private area, such as your office or a conference room with a closed door.

Your first sentence, after greeting them and asking them to sit, is to tell them they are being let go and that today is their last day. It may seem abrupt, but if you get that sentence out first the rest will go much easier, and the employee will have more time to absorb the news.

Step Two: Explain Why

Second, explain the reason why. Ideally the person won't be surprised, and this isn't the time to get into a debate, argument or to rehash all the details. Just state the basic reason succinctly. You might say something like, "As you know, we've been having performance issues related to the number of typos that are going out in your emails."

Step Three: Explain Next Steps

Step three, explain what happens next regarding the exit process. The details will vary of course based on your organization. You might review:

- When will they receive their final paycheck (often, by law, it must be on the same day of termination)?
- What is included in the final paycheck (e.g., unused paid-time-off, commissions, etc.)?
- What happens to their health benefits? Do they qualify for continuation under COBRA?
- Are you offering severance tied to a separation agreement?

Let them know that they'll probably have questions in the days and weeks ahead and they should contact you (or your HR department) at any time. Remember, anything you can do to reduce their anxiety will reduce the chance that they'll contact a lawyer or file a wrongful discrimination lawsuit.

Step Four: Gathering Their Things

Next, depending on your company policy, and the level of trust you have with the individual, you might explain that they will be escorted to gather their things or you can meet them outside of normal work hours to pack up.

Remember, not only do they need to gather their personal belongings, they need to return any company property that might be in their possession.

Step Five: Questions

Step five, ask them if they have any questions. Near the end, their minds may be reeling, so it's important to give them a minute to go over any points of confusion.

This is often the time when the employee will begin to probe further about the factors behind the termination. He might ask things like:

- How come I wasn't given more warning?

- Is this because I'm ____ (race, gender, age, religion, whatever)?
- Other people have made similar mistakes, so why am I the only one being fired?

While you want to clarify any potential misunderstandings, the termination meeting is not the right time or place to do so. This is the time when the employee's emotions will be highest and they won't have had time to process the information given. Just answer any of these types of questions with something like, "I'm happy to talk again about the reasons for our decision but not at this time. If you want to schedule time next week to talk again, that would be fine."

Step Six: Part On Good Terms

Finally, let them know that while it turned out the role wasn't right for them, you'd like to part on good terms. Let them know they can reach out with any questions in the days and weeks ahead. Offer to serve as a reference, if you are willing. You could offer to make them aware of any open positions you come across, and to reach out to your professional network for positions that might be a good fit for them.

While this extra step might not seem pleasant or necessary, you never know when a departing employee could end up working inside one of your client companies, or may even become the client. And at the very least, think about your company's brand and what they'll tell family and friends about how they were treated.

Sample Script When Firing Someone

Tailor your conversation to the specifics of your organization. Below is a sample of what you might say.

> *"Joe, we've decided to let you go and today is your last day. As we've discussed the last couple of months, your modules aren't passing quality standards in our code review.*
>
> *I want to explain some logistics of what happens next, and then answer any questions you have.*
>
> *Your final paycheck will include compensation for work up through today, and also payment for your unused paid-time-off. Your benefits will continue until the end of the calendar month, and you'll be eligible to keep your health insurance through COBRA, and HR can give you more details about that program.*
>
> *The company is offering you an additional four weeks of severance pay, in exchange for acceptance of this severance agreement. You'll want to read it carefully and may want to have an attorney review it before signing it.*
>
> *Before you leave, I'm going to need to collect your key card and laptop computer. In terms of your personal things in your office, I can walk with you to get them*

now, or I'd suggest maybe we could meet after work today or first thing tomorrow morning. It might be less disruptive and more private that way.

I know this is a lot to process, and I'll be available throughout the week to answer any questions. But do you have any questions now for me?

[Questions]

Joe, while it turned out this role wasn't right for you I want to leave on good terms. Anything I can do to help you to land your next position, just say the word."

I truly believe that the right way to tell someone they're being let go is also the nicest way, the most compassionate, and most professional. In the end, just treat the person as you would like to be treated if you were in their position.

We've decided to let you go, and today is going to be your last day.

CHAPTER #4

How To Write A Clear Termination Letter

How do you write a termination letter?

What should you put in it? And, what should you maybe leave out?

Before we get into the details, remember, employment law varies greatly by country and by state. This information doesn't replace the need for you to consult with your attorney or HR department about your specific situation.

A termination letter is just a written confirmation, for the person who is being let go. It puts down in writing the fact that the employee's position is being terminated and details the next steps in the process, like when they'll get their last paycheck, paid time off information, the status of their benefits and any instructions related to a severance agreement.

The letter is ideally drafted before you even notify the employee. This is so that you can use it to guide your in-person discussion.

Some state law requires written termination letters, most don't. But regardless of law, termination letters are considered best practice. While it might seem unnecessary, often when people hear the news they can get very emotional and overwhelmed. So they aren't in the best mindset to understand and to remember all the details that you are explaining. By having the letter ready to go during your meeting, you can hand it to them at the end, and they'll be able to go home and review all the details when they're ready.

There is a debate about whether termination letters should actually state the reason for dismissal. Some attorneys advise that the less that is put in writing, the better. But most seem to believe that stating the reason concisely—without going into the details—is the best approach and can help to avoid wrongful termination lawsuits.

Here's a sample of a typical termination letter:

Dear [EMPLOYEE NAME],

This letter confirms our discussion that your employment with [COMPANY NAME] is terminated for poor performance, effective immediately.

We have received from you already your security key card, your company credit card, company-owned laptop and cell phone at the termination meeting. According to our records you still possess a company-owned printer for your home office use; please return it in good condition to the company receptionist within 5 business days.

Your final paycheck is enclosed with this letter and it includes compensation for your accrued but unused paid time off (PTO).

You will receive two weeks' severance pay once you have signed and returned the enclosed release of claims document. You may pick up this check from the reception desk or we can mail it to your home.

You can expect a separate benefits status letter that will outline the status of eligibility for Consolidated Omnibus Budget Reconciliation Act (COBRA) continuation of group health coverage.

You will need to keep the company informed of your contact information so that we are able to provide the information you may need in the future such as your W-2 form. Please let us know if we can assist you during your transition.

Regards,

[Your name, position, company]

Of course, depending on your company's policies and benefits, the details of your letter may look very different.

Remember, even though writing a brief termination letter is an extra step in the process, it can go a long way to helping the exiting employee with their transition, and will reduce company risk.

CHAPTER #5

How To Fire Someone 'Nicely'

Everyone wants to know how to fire someone nicely, or how to fire someone gracefully. I'm often asked, how do you fire a friend? How do you fire someone with dignity?

There really is only one right way to let someone go (see Chapter 3). It's the best way, whether you like the person or not.

In the past, I (Kevin) made the mistake of trying to be nice by not really saying *why* they were being let go. I was vague, or said it isn't working out but it's the company's fault, anything I could do to make the other person not feel badly about himself. But it always backfired. Sometimes it dragged the process out longer. Sometimes they were confused. And if you're not direct with the person, you're actually robbing them of valuable feedback. This is feedback they can use to improve or at least find a job that fits their true strengths.

I've also made the mistake of agreeing to give the person just one more chance. They feel more stress than ever before, are now looking for another job as a backup, and the relationship between us is awkward. They always end up being fired anyway, or they resign once they land a new position.

And even in the best cases, they went away with valuable feedback–feedback that could lead them to a better next job...one that fits their talents better.

To fire someone nicely, just think about how you'd like to be treated if the roles were reversed. Realize that feedback can sometimes be painful, but it's always valuable.

- Be direct. The sooner you can say, "Hey, I'm sorry, but you're being let go and today is your last day," the better.

- Keep it short. Don't over explain. If you just got that news, wouldn't you want to get out of the office as quickly as possible to process the whole thing and to begin to think of next steps?

- Share the relevant next steps. Most people will want to know about their last paycheck, any commissions or unused paid time off, and how long will their healthcare insurance last.

- Let them know you're there for them and want to remain friends in the future. The right way to be nice is after the termination. Return their phone calls and emails quickly in the days and weeks ahead as they have questions about things. Reach out to your professional network and see if anyone has an opportunity for this person. Just because they didn't work out in YOUR company, or in that particular role doesn't mean they can't be successful somewhere else.

Conducting a termination is difficult, and it's harder when you like the person, or they've spent many years with the company. Just think about how you would like to be treated if the roles were reversed and let that be your guide.

"

Just think about how you'd like to be treated if the roles were reversed.

CHAPTER #6

When Is The Best Time To Fire Someone?

There is a lot of debate about when the best time is to fire an employee. Some argue Fridays are the only way to go, while others say it's not so much the actual day that matters as much as the time of day. Whatever your thoughts on the matter, any day and time you choose to fire someone will come with its own sets of advantages and hazards.

The Pros And Cons Of Friday

Not too long ago, it was standard practice to issue any terminations on Fridays, the theory being that it's easier for payroll and would give coworkers a few days to absorb the news and minimize disruption.

However, if you fire on Friday you've now given a terminated employee 48 hours to sit and stew; they aren't able to contact the unemployment office, or your HR department, and there's very little they can do for a job search on the weekend. Additionally, if you don't have time to talk to your remaining employees about the termination, rumors may spread and you'll have them updating their resume and changing their LinkedIn status over the weekend.

The Case For Monday's

Nowadays, the new normal is to terminate early in the week, notably even Monday mornings. It may seem a bit harsh to ask an employee to get up early, get ready, and commute into work on a day you'll be severing their employment, but it comes with certain advantages.

If they have any questions or confusion they can reach out over the course of the week, and they are far less likely to boil over during weekdays when they have the opportunity to reach out to their network for any leads, file for unemployment, and start to take steps in a new direction.

Monday also gives remaining employees a full week to get over any initial shock, plenty of time to ask questions, and a full five-day workweek to see that things are more or less normal.

What Time Of Day Should You Fire Someone?

Similar to the "which day" advice, the "what time" advice has changed in recent years.

Traditional wisdom is that you should fire someone at the end of the day so it minimizes disruption to the office. More recently people have been doing the opposite, and terminating employees in the morning. The rationale is that it gives the terminated employee a full day to process the information, ask questions, file for unemployment or review severance documents. Additionally, it gives management the rest of the day to notify employees and any outside parties that would need to know.

No One Right Answer

In the end, there is no one day or time that is better than another, although earlier in the week and earlier in the day has gained popularity.

The general consensus is that the best time to fire an employee is soon after you've reached the decision to do so, since delays can only invite complications and rumors.

> ***The best time to fire someone is always as quickly as possible after you've made up your mind to do so.***

CHAPTER #7

Can You Fire Someone Over The Phone?

Believe it or not, "Can I fire someone over the phone?" is one of the most common questions related to letting someone go. The short answer is, while it's not illegal to fire someone over the phone, most people considerate it to be unprofessional and it's not recommended.

This is because even though we now work in a world where digital communication is standard—with Slack, email, text messages—terminating someone's employment is not a normal message. And as uncomfortable as it might be for you to do it, you really owe it to the person involved to be face-to-face to maximize the quality of the communication.

There are a few exceptions in which firing someone over the phone would be considered OK. Perhaps you have a legitimate fear of physical or verbal assault, or maybe the person in question has been absent and not coming into work, or perhaps this person is a remote employee and you've never had an in person meeting before.

In these kinds of cases, pick the best communication channel available to you. A video conference app like Skype that enables you to talk face-to-face, would be better than a phone call. A phone call would be better than an email. An email would be better than a short text message.

> **It's not illegal to fire someone over the phone, just unprofessional.**

CHAPTER #8

Can You Fire Someone Without Warning?

There are times when you should definitely fire an employee immediately, without going through the normal escalation of warnings or performance conversations. Each case is unique but generally any acts of violence, threats of violence, harassment or theft would be valid reasons to terminate someone without warning.

And there are certainly times when you probably have a gut feeling, or out of anger or frustration, you *want* to take immediate action and nip the problem in the bud for the greater good. That being said, firing someone without any warning should be done rarely, since a sizable portion of employees who end up filing wrongful termination lawsuits are doing so because the reason for their termination was not made clear to them. Before you do anything rash, here's what you need to consider before firing someone without warning.

Consider Their Contract

Look over their employment contract (or union agreement should that apply) carefully. There may be binding language that keeps your hands tied in one way or another, and it's better to find out now than when you get a call from a lawyer. If need be, inquire with HR about the details and any federal or national laws that may intercede.

Determine If They Are "At Will"

An "at will" employee is employed under the premise that their position may be terminated at any point, and without a reason (although, as we've explored before, it's best to outline the reason). This also means that employees have the freedom to quit without reason and at any time.

If your company is located in an "at will" state and the employee contract indicates they are an "at will" hire, then technically there is nothing stopping you from firing them without notice. However…

Just Because It's Legal, Doesn't Mean It's Right

Here's the rub: if an employee is truly surprised by their termination, chances are you have not done your part as a manager. Unless their behavior crosses over into physical violence, harassment there is a good chance they are unaware of their behavior or the fact they may be underperforming.

A good manager needs to sit down with troubled employees and issue warnings—behavioral guardrails, if you will—and give them a real shot at improving or correcting the issues you've brought up. If, after a few warnings, they have not made an effort to better themselves and are continuing to make the rest of your team uncomfortable, then you can terminate them with the confidence that you gave them a fair shake.

Remember, your goal with an employee termination isn't just to remove the employee. It should also be to minimize disruption to the work environment, minimize the risk of an unlawful termination lawsuit, and if possible, to preserve a positive relationship with the departing employee.

"
Acts of violence, threats of violence, harassment or theft would be valid reasons to terminate someone without warning.

CHAPTER #9

Is It Possible To Fire Someone For No Reason?

Employment law varies by country and by state. You should consult with a local employment attorney for your specific situation. This book doesn't replace good legal counsel; consider it solid background information based on real-world experience and it will help you to explore HR issues with your lawyers more effectively.

Most states are considered "at will employment" states, which means unless indicated otherwise (in their employment agreement or union rules), employers may fire employees for no reason, or for any reason (as long as that reason doesn't fall into the illegal reasons as described previously). Likewise, an employee may quit for no or for any reason; it works both ways.

However, as previously stated, you increase your risk of a wrongful termination lawsuit if you don't offer a reason for the termination. If no reason is given, it's only natural that the person in question will begin to wonder if it has something to do with their gender, race, age, religion or other illegal discriminatory factors.

> **Just because you can, doesn't mean you should.**

BONUS

Employee Termination Checklist

Whether you are letting someone go for budgetary, performance, or other reasons, you want the difficult process be as professional and smooth as possible. This comprehensive termination checklist will keep you on track.

❏ **Step One: Review**

Meet with your boss and Human Resources representative to review the legal reason for termination, any warnings that may have been issued, and the details of their exit (including last paycheck, benefit information, possible severance) and plan to cover the work and replace the employee.

❏ **Step Two: Write a Termination Letter**

An official letter provides a more formal notification of their termination and includes all of the details related to final paycheck, benefits and possible severance.

❏ **Step Three: Coordinate**

Coordinate with your security department if you plan to have the employee escorted from the premises or fear that the employee may become violent. Coordinate with IT so they'll know when to cut off access to email and other computer services. Coordinate in confidence, and carefully, with any other employees who may need to prepare ahead of time.

❏ **Step Four: Tell Them**

Choose a private place, like your office or conference room, to have a face-to-face meeting. Tell the employee, "We've decided to let you go, and today will be your last day here." You can share the reason but keep it concise and don't let it turn into a debate. Focus on what happens next with their final paycheck, benefits, and possible severance.

❏ **Step Five: Collect Property**

Collect any company property including: ID badge, office keys, laptop or other computer equipment, mobile phone, and company credit card.

❏ Step Six: Walk Them Out

Have them escorted to their desk so they can gather their personal things and then walk them out of the building. Alternatively, to minimize office disruption and give them more privacy, suggest you can meet them at the end of the day or before work starts on the following day for them to collect their things.

❏ Step Seven: Notify Employees & Outside Parties

As soon as possible, meet with any employees who are affected by the departure and let them know that the person was let go. Let them know that due to employee confidentiality reasons, you can't give specifics, but they weren't performing to standards required in the job (or they weren't the right fit for that role). You want to make sure people know they weren't let go as part of a lay-off, unless they were. Use this meeting to discuss anticipated plans to replace them and who covers the work until a replacement is found.

❏ Step Eight: Support

In the week's following the termination, answer any questions the employee has and offer career support if possible (e.g., letter of recommendation, reach out to your professional network to see if anyone has relevant openings, etc.)

FREE Management Training

At LEADx, we give busy managers FREE leadership training videos, every single day. Learn how to...

Increase Employee Engagement

Tame Your Email Inbox

Run Effective Meetings

Give Effective Feedback

More!

Get Your Free Training

www.LEADx.org

LEADx MANAGEMENT TRAINING

Bring the Power of LEADx Training to Your Organization

How can you quickly and easily give your front-line managers the critical skills they need to be successful? How can you turn your managers into effective coaches? How can your managers learn to run effective meetings and to master their burdensome email inbox? LEADx solutions include:

- LEADxAcademy online learning system
- LEADxGuide books for busy managers
- Keynote speeches and workshops consultants

Email info@LEADx.org

Call 267-756-7089

Visit us on the web at www.LEADx.org

About the Authors

Kevin Kruse is the Founder and CEO of LEADx, a keynote speaker, and a *New York Times* best-selling author of *Employee Engagement 2.0* and *15 Secrets Successful People Know About Time Management*.

Tara Millette, Editor at LEADx, oversees all content production for the LEADx website, hosts live training shows, and co-hosts the weekly LEADx podcast. Prior to LEADx, Tara's writing covered everything from stand-up comedy to political satire.

How To Fire An Employee Copyright © 2017 by LEADx Inc.

All rights reserved. No part of this publication may be reproduced, stored in a retrieval system, or transmitted by any means – electronic, mechanical, photographic (photocopying), recording, or otherwise – without prior permission in writing from the author. This book contains articles that were previously published as part of the author's blog on kevinkruse.com, Forbes.com, or other online forums, but have been revised and updated since the date of their original publication.

This book is for entertainment purposes only. The views expressed are those of the author alone, and should not be taken as expert instruction or commands or substitute for legal advice. The reader is responsible for his or her own actions. Adherence to all applicable laws and regulations is the sole responsibility of the purchaser or reader. Neither the author nor the publisher assumes any responsibility or liability whatsoever on the behalf of the purchaser or reader of these materials. Any perceived slight of any individual or organization is purely unintentional.

Tradepaper ISBN-13: 978-0-9993899-0-4

Printed in Great Britain
by Amazon

54326181R00036

Smalltalk bytes book

1st edition

Eric Tatham

A Mixed Reality Publication

Mixed Reality Limited
40 Bawnmore Road
Rugby
Warwickshire
CV22 7QN

Website: www.MixedReality.co.uk
email: etatham@MixedReality.co.uk

Copyright © Eric Tatham 2003

The right of Eric Tatham to be identified as the author of this work has been asserted by him in accordance with the Copyright, Designs and Patents Act 1988.

All rights reserved. No part of this publication may be reproduced or transmitted in any form or by any means, electronic or mechanical, including photocopy, recording, or any information storage and retrieval system, without either the prior wriiten permission of the Publisher or a licence permitting restricted copying in the United Kingdom issed by the Copyright Licensing Agency Limited, 90 Tottenham Court Road, London W1P 9HE.

First published 2003

ISBN 0-9544514-0-6

Digitally printed in England by George Over Ltd., Rugby, Warwickshire.

Preface

This book is intended as a tutorial reference guide for students studying object-oriented programming using Smalltalk. It is organised in glossary form, rather than as a tutorial to be worked through from beginning to end. This inevitably means that some topics can appear under more than one heading so, where this occurs, cross references are provided. I have also compiled a general index so that terms and method names can be found, even if they do not warrant a main glossary entry in their own right. The decision to treat the material in this way was prompted by requests for such a reference text from my tutees on the Open University undergraduate course; *M206, Computing: An Object-Oriented Approach*.

I have written with Open University students in mind and hence used illustrative examples based on the LearningWorks™ environment from Neometron Inc.. However, LearningWorks™ is based on VisualWorks™ from Cincom Systems Inc., and almost all of the book's content is applicable to any Smalltalk environment. (See the entry under *Smalltalk* for further details.)

I have used `Courier` typeface for variable names and for Smalltalk code, and a **Sans Serif** font for class names. Where class names represent abstract classes, they are shown in italics.

I hope you enjoy the book and find it useful, and can excuse any mistakes that remain.

Eric Tatham
(2003)